MINI PRISON CELLS

Eric "Superman" Sturgess

Rose Of Sharon
PUBLISHING

ERIC "SUPERMAN" STURGESS

Printed Worldwide
First Printing 2025
First Edition 2025

10 9 8 7 6 5 4 3 2 1

Rose of Sharon Publishing books may be ordered through booksellers or by contacting:

Rose Of Sharon Publishing
roseofsharonpublishing.com
P.O. Box 186
Floresville, Texas 78114

ISBN: 978-1-967791-95-8 Paperback

Dedication

This book is a heartfelt dedication to the men in the California Department of Corrections and Rehabilitation, as well as those in prisons across America, who are striving to improve themselves and reunite with their loved ones. Within the confines of those prison walls, many men have been blessed with remarkable talents, and they take great pride in their creations and the stories they have to share. This humble book serves as a platform for their voices to be heard.

I have taken it upon myself to write numerous letters of support for resentencing and parole board hearings on behalf of my incarcerated friends in the California Department of Corrections and Rehabilitation. I am fully committed to assisting in their release, and these letters of support play a crucial role in that endeavor.

"The Lord has given them special skills as engravers, designers, embroiderers in blue, purple, and scarlet thread on fine linen cloth, and weavers. They excel as craftsmen and as designers," Exodus 35:35.

God bless you,
Eric "Superman" Sturgess
Psalm 91

Preface

Miniature prison cell models made by convicts in the California Department of Corrections and Rehabilitation are rare to find. Decades ago, they were more commonly made, but by 2025, they had become a thing of the past. I have talked to numerous convicts behind the walls, and most of them tell me they don't see them being made.

Some of the more complex ones can take over six months to make. Acquiring all of the parts necessary to construct a complete miniature prison cell is a herculean task. The entire process is too expensive and time-consuming, so that is probably the main reason this form of arts and crafts in prison is almost extinct.

Another thing to consider is that they still have to get the miniature prison cell out of the prison without it breaking during the shipping process. The prison cells are very fragile, and many of the intricate pieces throughout the cells fall off the walls and shelves, breaking. Ask me how I know this? I have seven of these miniature prison cells in my art collection. They are probably my most prized artifacts from behind the prison walls in the California Department of Corrections and Rehabilitation.

I hope you enjoy these rare pictures and appreciate the time and effort that went into making them. They are impressive creations that required considerable skill and dedication to create.

God bless you
Eric Sturgess
Romans 10:9-13

Foreword

Prison cells are what society and our government created to isolate, punish, and deter criminals from committing crimes. They are as old as history itself, and only those who have spent time in them know the feeling that is felt when the doors close behind them. Creating a replica of a prison cell is a challenging task. One of the most difficult steps in making them is gathering all the necessary materials to assemble them. They are not like the model car sets that can be purchased online or at a hobby store. They don't come with all the parts in a box, nor do they include directions to follow. To create these cell models, individuals need to possess skill, patience, and creativity.

Although prison cells are somewhat similar in layout, each convict artist builds their own replica of the cell according to the prison in which they are housed. Prison cells differ in their dimensions, the content inside, and the type of door construction. For instance, cell doors in prisons, which are considered Level IV-180 and Level IV-270 maximum security prisons, tend to have honeycomb doors that allow officers to look inside the cell from different angles within the buildings. The cell doors can be opened and closed with the push of a button by the officer in the control booth. Level III prisons have solid metal doors with a small window and a food tray slot located in the lower center. In contrast, in old prisons such as Folsom, San Quentin, and Chino, cell doors are made of iron bars.

Some prison cells are smaller than others, depending on when they were constructed and the intended security level of the occupants. For instance, cells in the Pelican Bay Security Housing Unit are big, while cells in prisons such as Folsom and San Quentin are relatively smaller.

All the above things need to be considered as they play a role in the creation of a cell replica. When the artist sets out to create a replica of their cells, the first thing they do is take measurements of their cells. This helps them develop replicas as precisely as possible. Of course, convicts are not professional architects, but they are certainly creative. The walls for the cells can be made out of materials such as checkerboards, cardboard, rolled-up paper, or Styrofoam boards that can be purchased through the prison's catalogues in the hobby craft programs.

The material can also be found in certain areas within the prison, such as the school, vocational area, or dayrooms. Some convicts carve appliances, sinks, and toilets out of PIA soap. Others use checkerboards, popsicle sticks, or the thin cardboard from the back of our writing tablets to create them.

The clothes, such as towels, bed sheets, blankets, shirts, and pants that are seen inside the lockers, can be made out of paper, or if the artist is bold, he will cut off pieces of his own clothes, blanket, and linen to make such items look as real as possible. Cutting pieces out of state-issued clothes can lead to an RVR (Rules Violation Report). They can be punished with a 30-day loss of privileges and may even be charged for the damage to state property. The paint, glue, and wax used to detail the items in the cells, such as floors, walls, lockers, bunks, toilets, and appliances, can be obtained through hobby craft programs or art classes. Suppose those items can't be obtained through the ways above. In that case, the artist will likely get them from his peers who work in vocational areas, maintenance buildings, plant operations, or even at the program office. Convicts are prohibited from possessing acrylic paint, as it is a flammable item that can compromise the safety and security of the institution.

As you will see in the pages of this book, some artists actually install real LED lights and electrical systems that open and close the cell doors with the push of a button. They do this by utilizing wires from their headphone cable extensions and motors from their old CD players. To create such an intricate and amazing feature, the convict will need to have some knowledge of electrical systems. The artist will need to know what type of wire to use and select the correct CD player motor. CD players contain two small motors, known in prison slang as the "pancake" (large) or "Jolly Rancher" (small) type.

These motors operate at different voltages, and their power levels differ from one another. To set up the electrical system, the wires must be run through the walls, and a battery system must be placed either on top of the cell door, under the cell, or on the back of the cell. Replica cells have been made for decades in the California Department of Corrections and Rehabilitation. I have spent over 20 years in prison, and I have made numerous miniature cells in that time for my friends and family.

My cell is my temporary home, and it's where I spend most of my time. Therefore, I care about how it looks, how it smells, and how organized it is. When officers conduct random or targeted cell searches, they often comment on the cleanliness or dirtiness of the cells.

Some correctional officers tend to appreciate cells that are clean and organized. Moreover, many of them show respect to convicts who know how to maintain their cells in an orderly manner. Temporary placement is what these cells are for us, so from my cell to the world, I say, enjoy this book.

Isaac Morquecho

Table of Contents

Dedication....................3
Preface....................4
Foreword....................5
Photographs....................9
About the Author....................47
Other Books....................50

Photographs

This cell is a miniature replica of a cell at Richard J. Donovan State Prison. This model is 10x10x8 inches. It took the artist six months to finish. The cell door opens with a push of a button and this model has working lights powered by four AA

OFF
ON
CHASE LIGHT
PUSH/PULL THE LEVER OPEN TO VIEW INSIDE THE CELL
16
124
A2B
A1A
DPM/DNH
125
C-C
LOP
A2B
DLT

ERIC "SUPERMAN" STURGESS

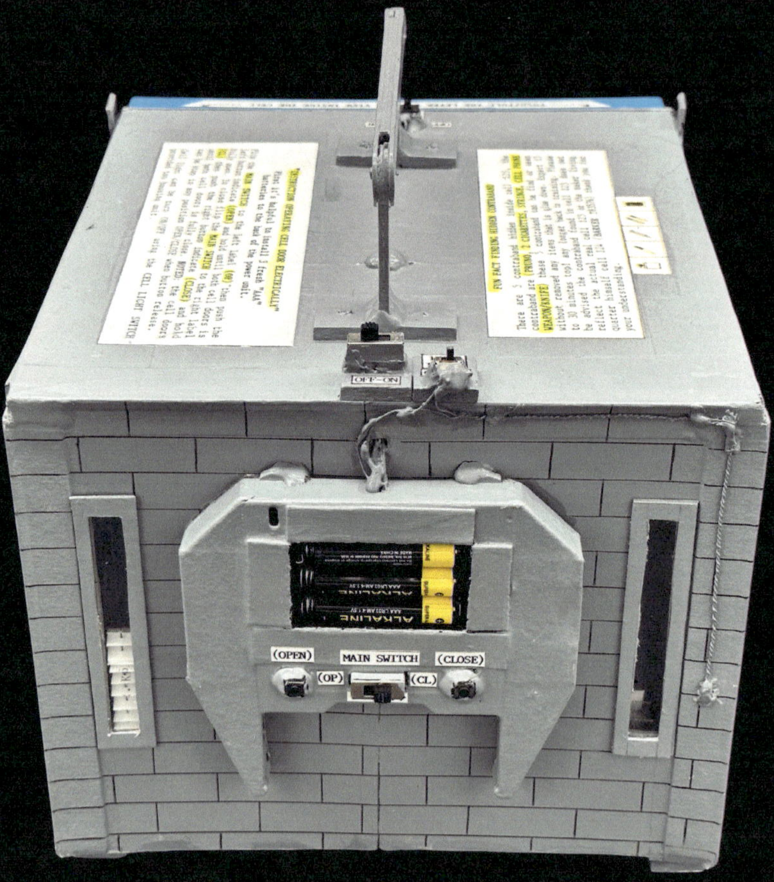

ERIC “SUPERMAN” STURGESS

16
124
A2B
A1A
DPM/DNH
C-C
LOP
A2B
DLT
125
2025

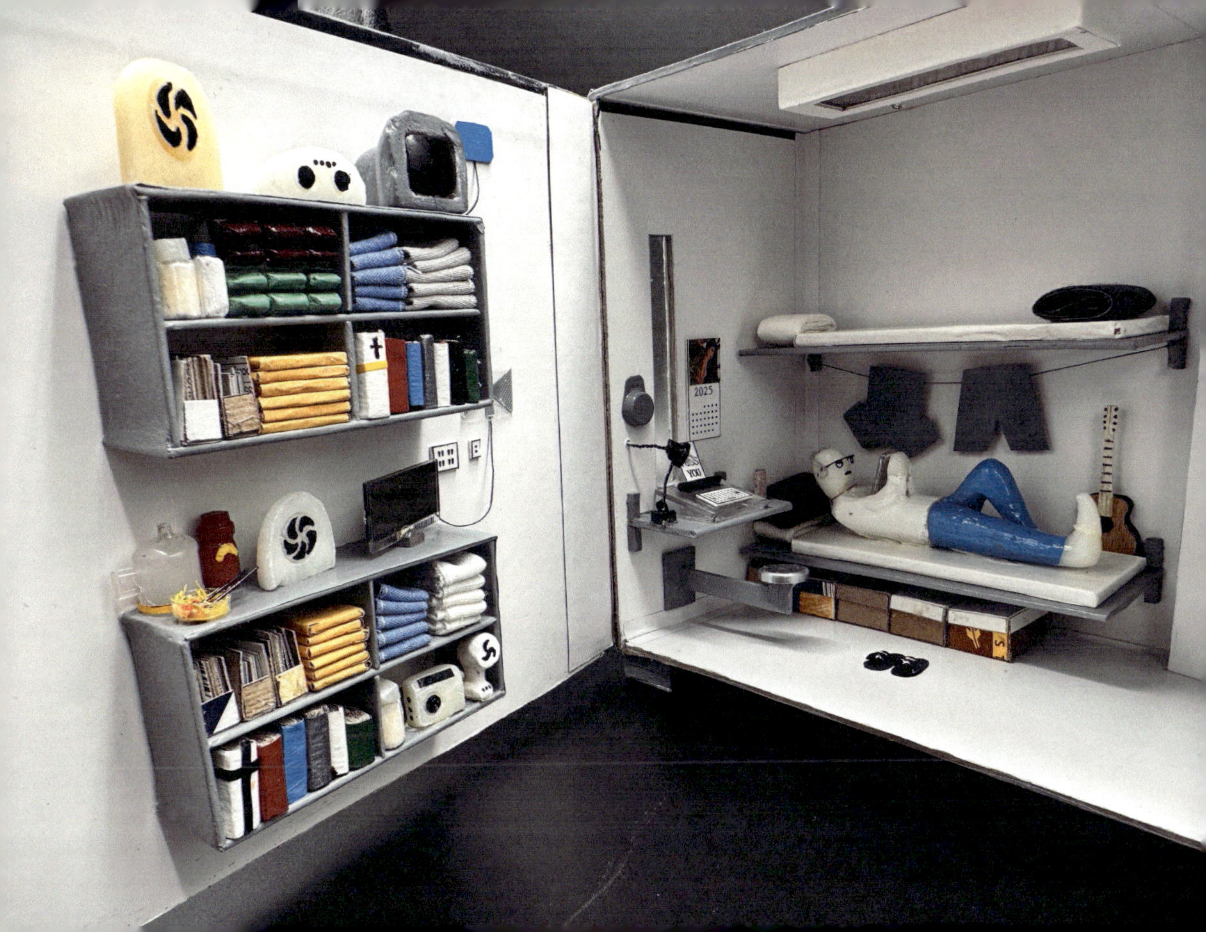
2025
YOU

2025
YOU

ERIC “SUPERMAN” STURGESS

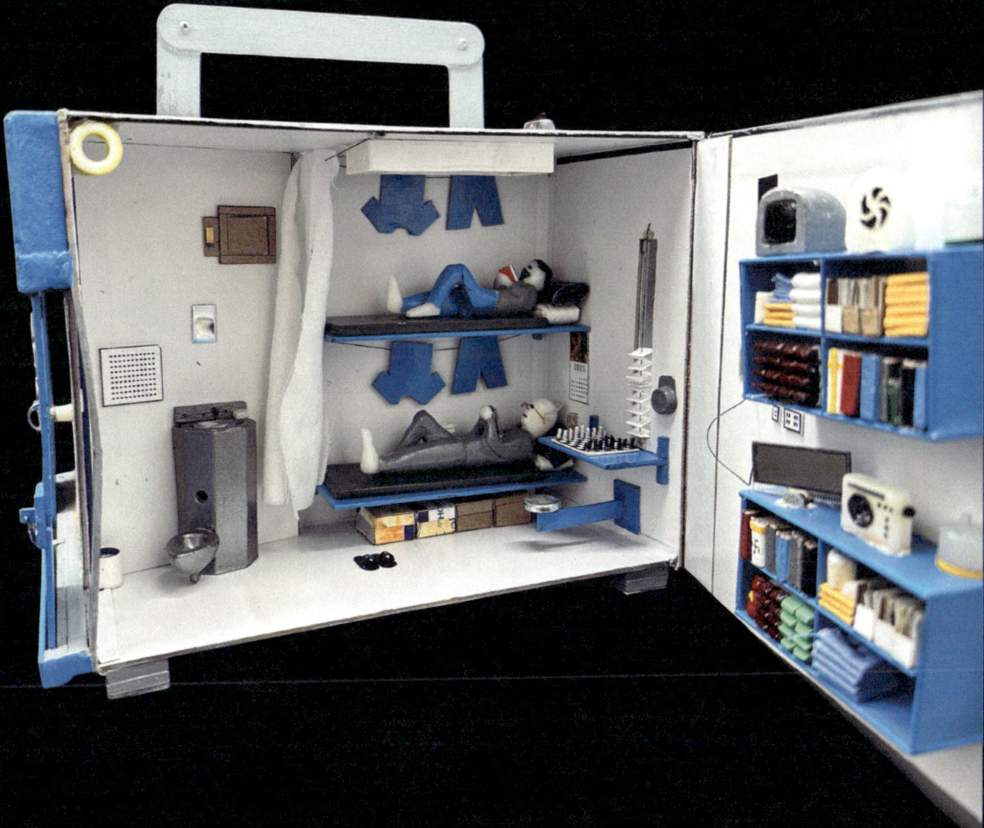

2025

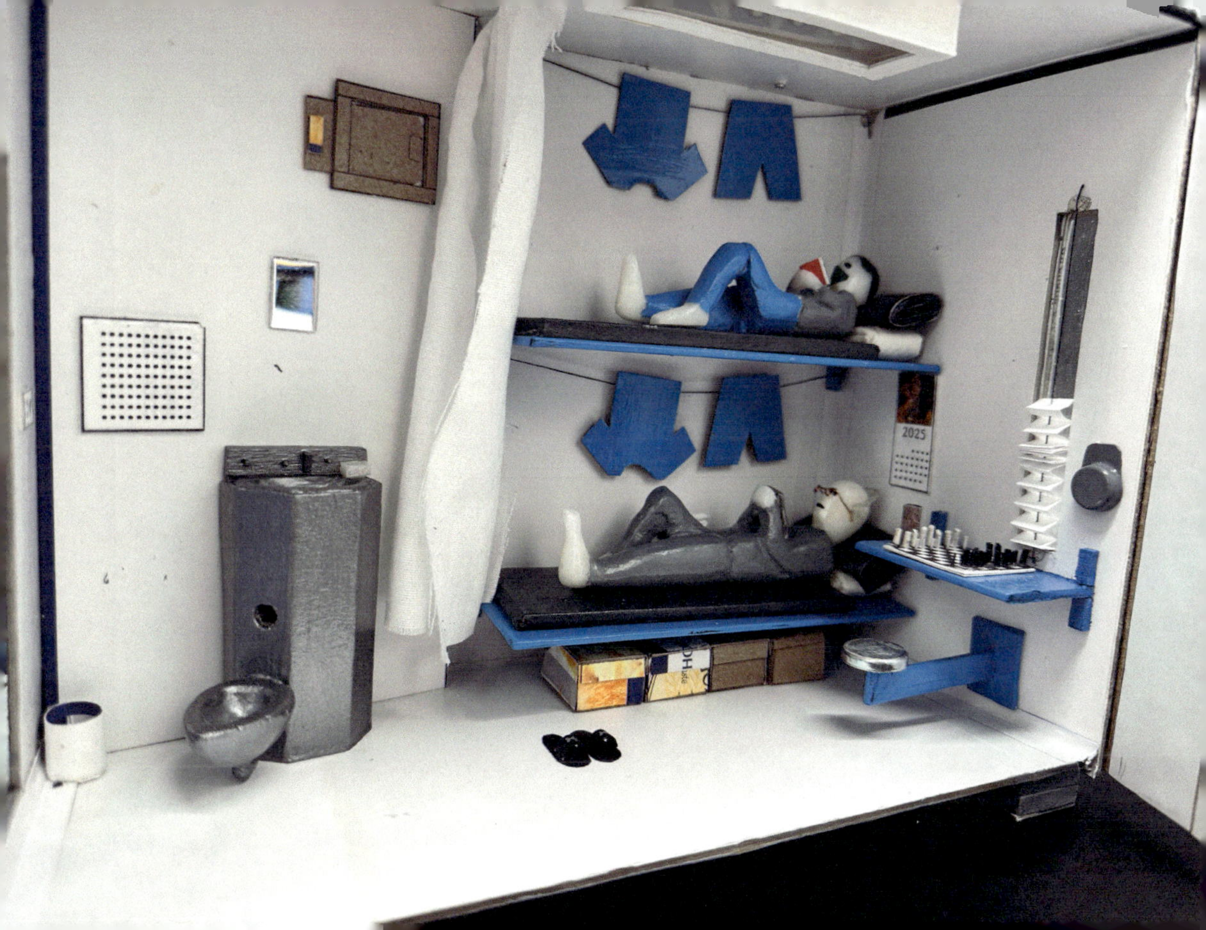
2025

This model is a replica of a prison cell at Folsom State Prison. It measures 5x10x10 inches.

ERIC "SUPERMAN" STURGESS

ERIC “SUPERMAN” STURGESS

ERIC "SUPERMAN" STURGESS

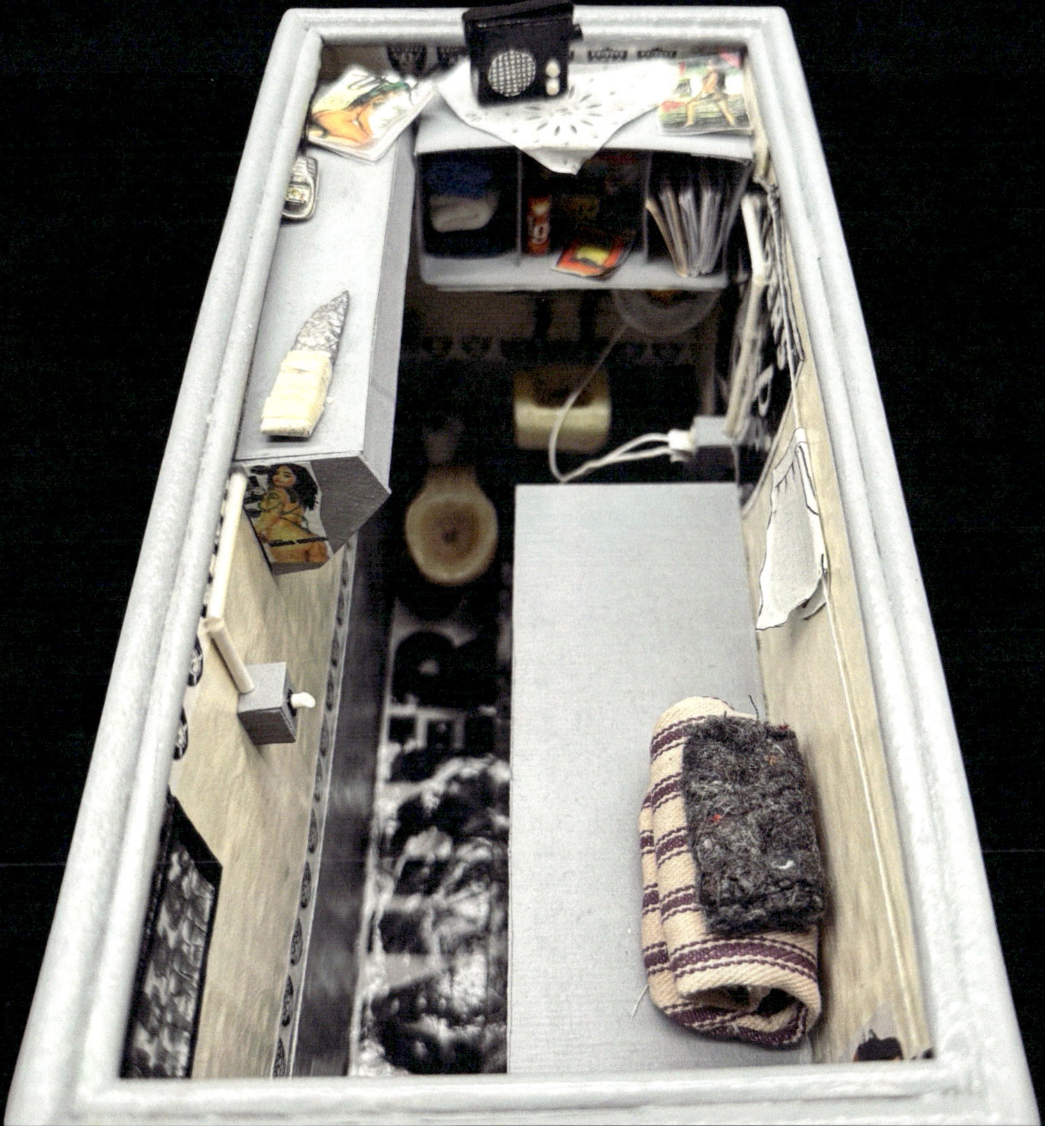

This cell is a miniature replica of a cell at Richard J. Donovan State Prison. This model is 4x8x8 inches. The cell door opens with a push of a button and this model has working lights powered by four AA batteries.

DEPARTMENT OF CORRECTIONS AND REHABILITATION
STATE OF CALIFORNIA
2024
245
A2B
I-W
A1A
IDL

DEPARTMENT OF CORRECTIONS AND REHABILITATION
STATE OF CALIFORNIA
245
A2B
I-W
A1A
IDL

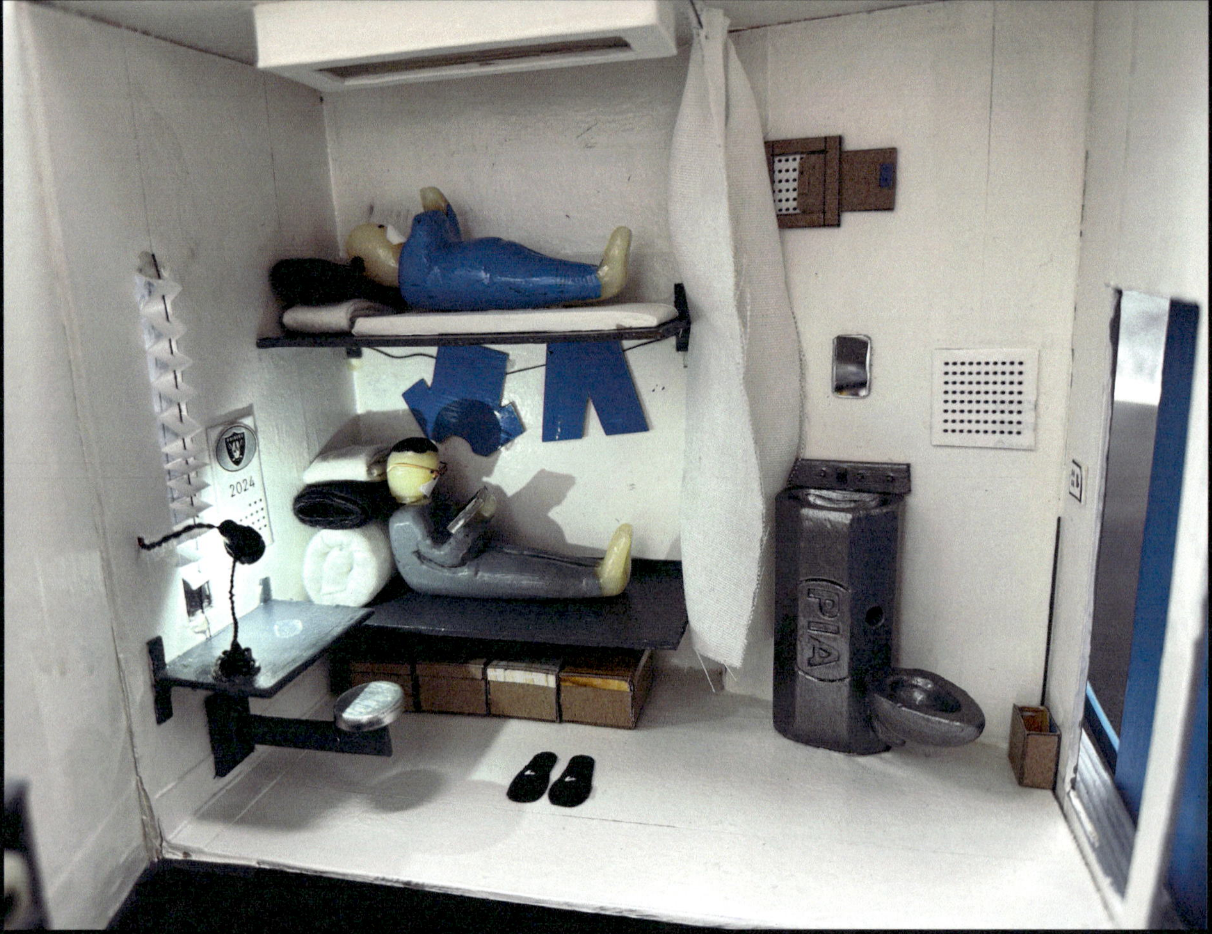
2024
PIA

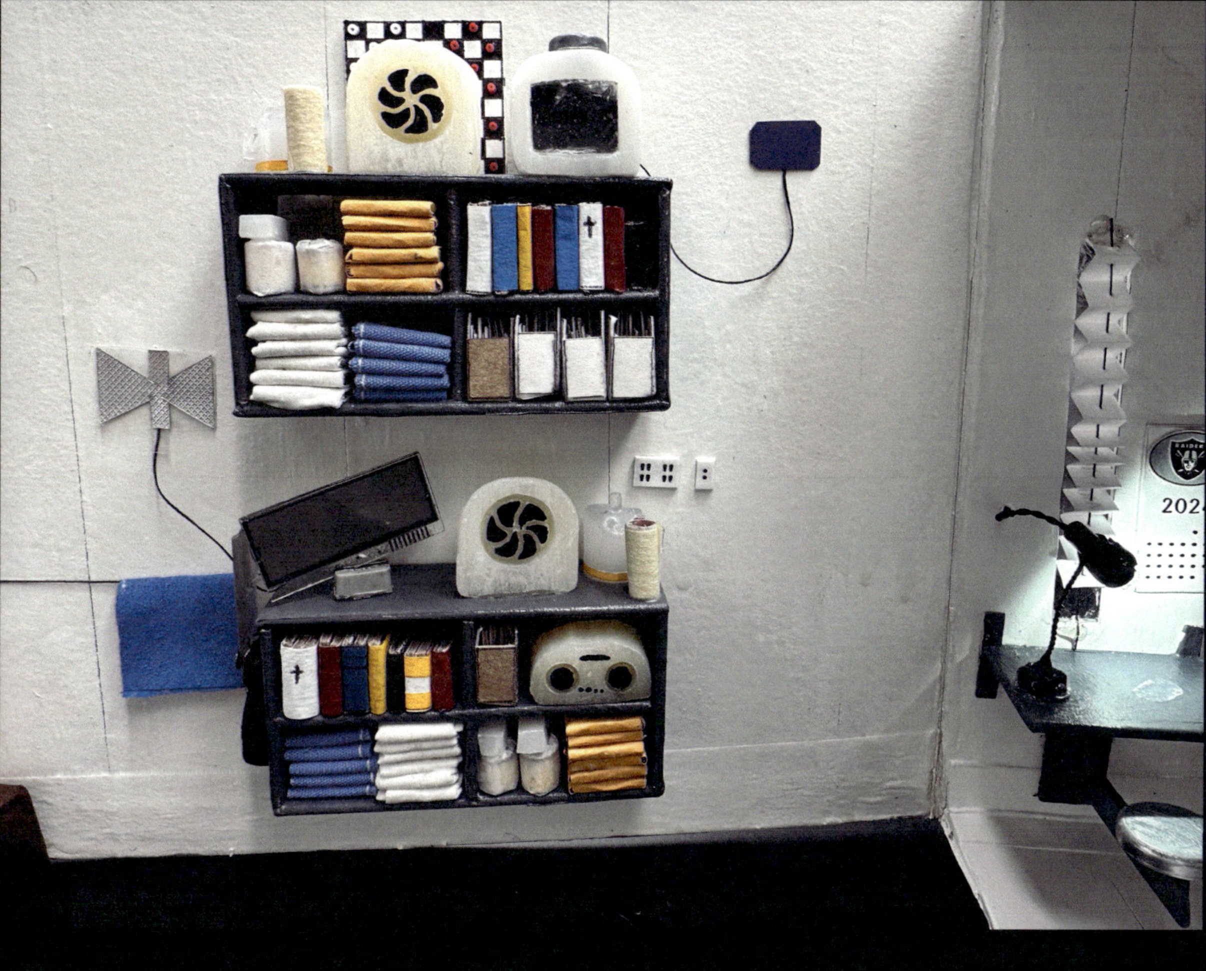

This model is a replica of a prison cell at Lancaster State Prison. It measures 8x8x9 inches. The artist who made it is David Estrada, CDC#H94762, Facility Bravo, Building 1, Cell 232 Lower.

Jazz
PLAYER
Marlboro
Dove
Colgate

This model is a replica of a prison cell at Folsom State Prison. It measures 7x7x11 inches.

ERIC “SUPERMAN” STURGESS

Folsom Prison

ERIC "SUPERMAN" STURGESS

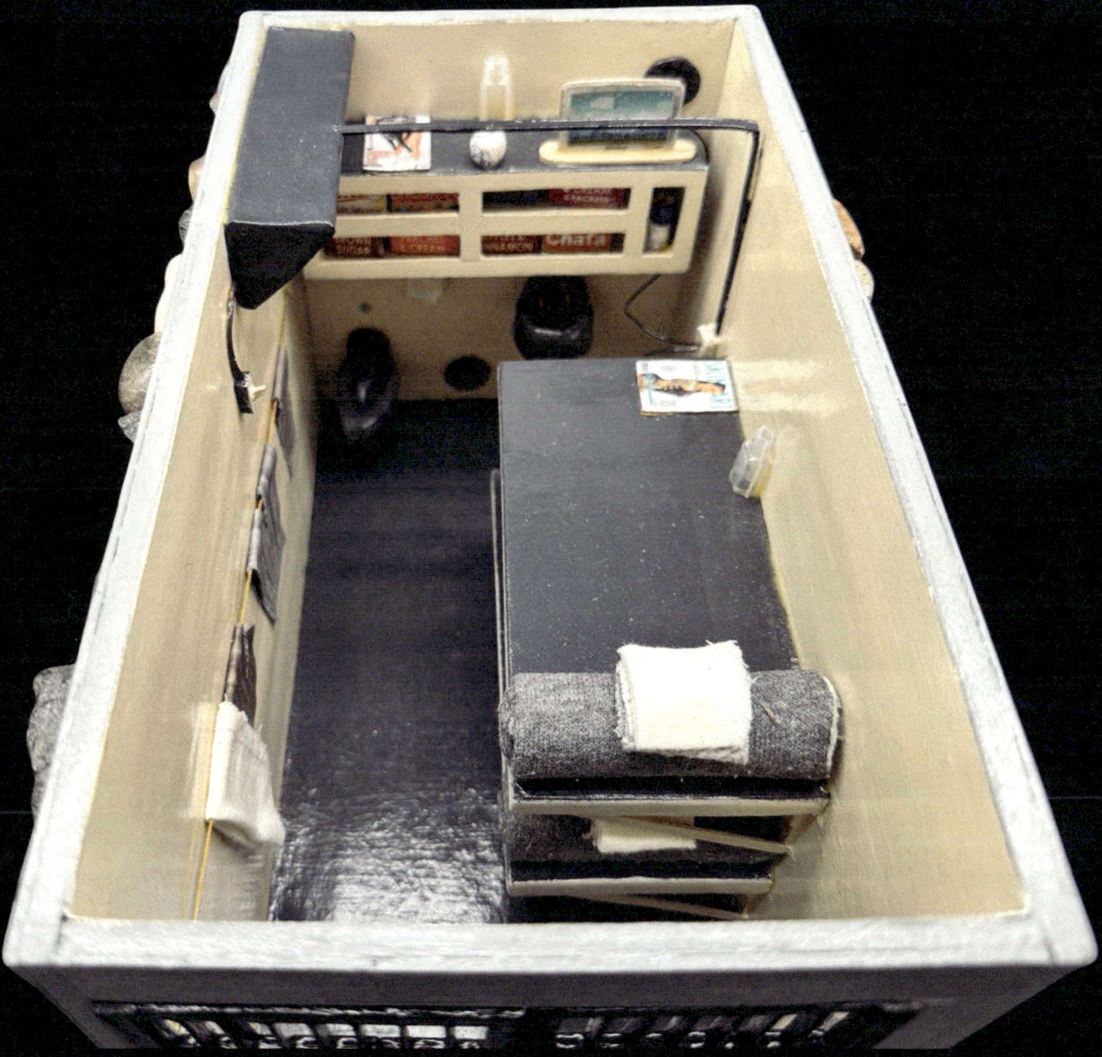

SKIN ART

This model is a replica of a Death Row prison cell at San Quentin State Prison. It measures 5x10x10 inches. The artist is Morris Solomon CDC#H50300. He was known as the Sacramento Slayer and he was a serial killer.

This model is a replica of a prison cell at Centinela State Prison. It measures 6x6x8 inches.

WBOYS
QUAKER
Jelly Belly
GARLIC

About the Author

Eric has emerged as a highly accomplished investor and Day Trader, engaging in trading activities with a substantial value of stocks annually. He enjoys the status of a dedicated husband and father, being blessed with four wonderful daughters who hold a special place in his heart. Eric's existence revolves around upholding the virtues of a devout Christian, a devoted husband, and a caring father guided by the grace of God. His journey has been transformative, considering his challenging upbringing, and he now stands as an illustrious testament to the boundless possibilities achievable through faith in God.

Eric joined a criminal street gang as a teenager, and he was eventually arrested and put in a cage at the Long Beach City Jail. He dropped out of Jordan High School in Long Beach, California, in the 10th grade. Eric eventually got on the right path by the grace of God and obtained his GED the same month that he would have graduated. He joined the United States Coast Guard at 18, and after four years of faithful service, he was honorably discharged.

The following is an excerpt from his autobiography: "California Prison Confessions." "It was a typical beautiful summer night in Long Beach, California, and the three young teens fighting in the musty garage starkly contrasted the night's serenity. A teen called Bones was thrown against a wall, and a muscular teenager nicknamed E Double (me) rushed towards him and violently punched him in his lower back. Another youth named Tim Loc held Bones against the wall during this attack. E Double's knuckles landed with a thick-sounding thud as Bones grimaced and moaned in pain from each successive blow.

There's a look of pain and fear in Bone's eyes as E Double mercilessly lands blow after blow to his kidneys. E Double has spent years hitting the heavy bag in his garage, so his punches are devastating for his age. The beating lasted a minute, and the two teens stopped attacking the unfortunate victim. Amazingly, they all shook hands and embraced each other. We were all friends, and this was our modest gang initiation into our small clique called 'Six Feet Under.'"

Our tiny neighborhood gang in North Long Beach, California, had several members of various races: White, Black, and Hispanic. The definition of a criminal street gang according to the California Penal Code is as follows: "As used in this chapter, 'criminal street gang' means any ongoing organization, association, or group of three or more persons, whether formal or informal, having as one of its primary activities the commission of one or more of the criminal acts…having a common name or common identifying sign or symbol, and whose members individually or collectively engage in or have engaged in a pattern of criminal gang activity," California Penal Code 186.22(f).

Some of our associates committed serious crimes such as burglaries, drug sales, stealing cars, carrying guns, vandalism, and assaulting people. Although we were nothing but young punks, we were a criminal street gang according to the California Penal Code.

The FBI did a study entitled "Street-Gang Mentality: A Mosaic of Remorseless Violence and Relentless Loyalty." I want to quote a relevant part concerning young males who do not have a father or other positive male role models in their lives while growing up: "All gang members lacked male role models in their households, and when they lived with their mothers, they were rarely home because of work schedules. Gang members often lived temporarily with various people. All but one gang member reported that one or more immediate family members had a criminal history or abused drugs. Gangs attracted them because of their loyalty, stability, and sense of group identity."

There is an epidemic in this country of boys masquerading as men who don't take their responsibilities as fathers seriously. Many fathers aren't involved in their children's lives; if they are, they are a horrible example of what a real man should be. One of the main factors in young men ending up in the penal system is the lack of a father or, at the very least, a positive male role model when they were growing up. Absentee fathers are causing society to pay a high price for their selfish and callous actions.

Every day, I strive to be the best dad to the four beautiful daughters God has blessed me with. I live by the motto, "Be the man you needed as a child." I will not allow the actions of physically and emotionally abusive people to define who I am or hinder my advancement in life. You can choose to be bitter or better. I strive for excellence because living well is the best response to abusive people.

Eric Sturgess

God bless you and yours.

Romans 10:9-13

For those seeking to connect with Eric or gather additional insights about his upcoming projects, please visit his official website: EricSturgess.com.

Other Books

Prison Paños: Ink On Cloth

Prison Art Paños

Prison Art Hats

California Prisons:
Boxing Program History

Mini Prison Cells

California Prison Polaroids

Camp Mendenhall: California Juvenile Detention Camp

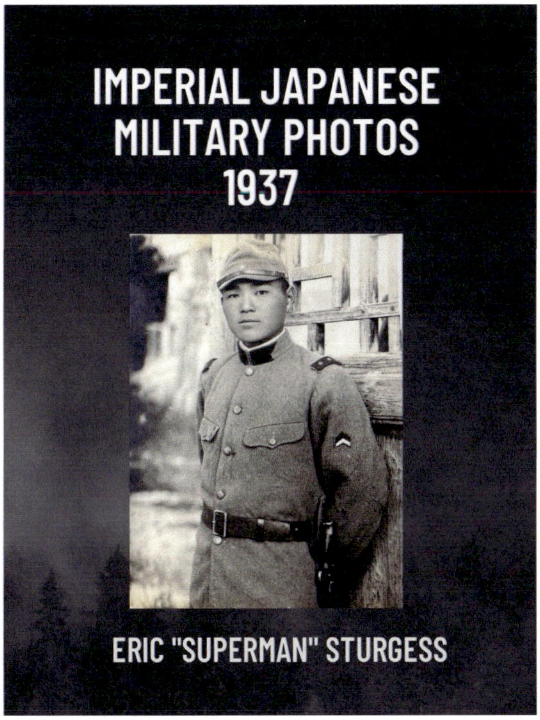

Imperial Japanese Military Photos 1937

Prison Art Envelopes

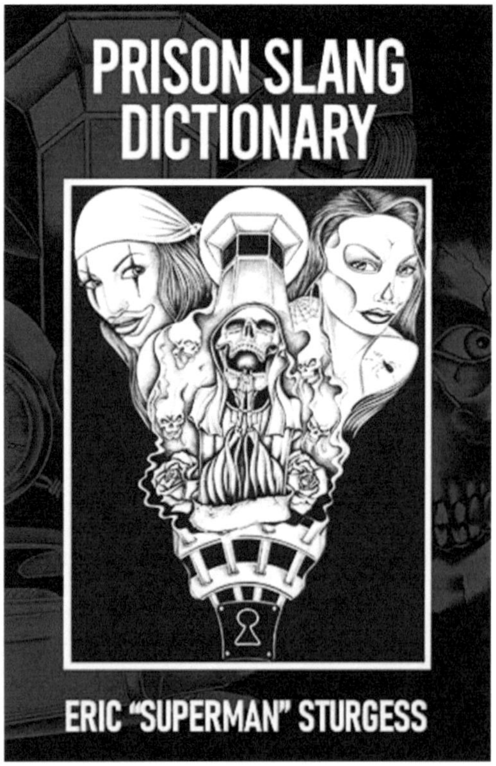

Prison Slang Dictionary

Made in the USA
Monee, IL
05 November 2026

67378694R00033